Whiskey

© 2003 Feierabend Verlag OHG

Mommsenstraße 43

D-10629 Berlin

Project management: Bettina Freeman

Translation from German: Heather Stacey, Edinburgh

Editing of the English edition: Lizzie Gilbert, Cologne

Typesetting: Roman Bold & Black, Cologne

Overall concept and co-ordination: Redaktionsbüro Udo Pini, Hamburg

Picture editing: Nicola Kossel, Hamburg

Design: Isabel Böcking, Hamburg

Lithography: kölnermedienfabrik, Cologne

Printing and binding: Poligratici Calderara s.p.a., Bologna

Printed in Italy

ISBN 3-936761-55-8

61-04014-1

Udo Pini

Whiskey

Feierabend

Conte

nts

sky or whiskey?

Scottish whisky was first spelt "whiskey" in 1715.
the beginning of the 20th century the Irish had
stomed themselves to this spelling. However,
cots still use "whisky", as do the Canadians, the
ese and many other countries with their own
ction. Only the USA, the bourbon superpower,
the Irish in using the "-ey" spelling. In this book
ky" and "whiskey" are used where appropriate
or fairness, "whisk^{e}y" is used for general points.

Slainté, Sho

slaynt, Cheers!

There are few high-proof drinks as highly regarded world-wide as whisk^ey. The Irish and Scots had been producing it for centuries and eventually shared their pure distilled treasure and toasting expressions with the rest of the world. Connoisseurs delight in the subtleties of the amber nectar, such as the depth of the aroma or the unique character of a single cask malt. Purists make distinctions based on water quality, the shape of the still and the microclimate in the warehouse. All aficionados decide early on whether their preference is for peaty Scotch whiskies, milder Irish whiskeys, softer Canadians, or sweet US whiskeys with vanilla notes. And many people swear by the secret blend formula of their favorite brand.

Role models

Bronson Dudley and Steve Buscemi brood over their bourbon, Pamela Anderson mulls things over with a Wild Turkey, Charles favors Prince of Wales, Harvey Keitel calms his fury with whiskey, and John Ritter seeks solace at the bar in "Skin Deep". Whiskey offers support and style, because its drinkers are in a class of their own. Whenever whiskey is served or celebrated it immediately adds another layer of intensity to a film scene. Whiskey lovers are never hurried and always relish an independent spirit.

Unbeatable

The stakes are high between Ernie Kovacs and Alec Guinness when they play chess with 32 miniatures in "Our Man in Havana": Irish pawns against Scottish ones, the malt knights against the bourbon castles – and the Canadian Queen threatening the Scottish King. The winner takes it all, but then it is his turn to buy. Countless films depict the whiskey ritual of being bought a drink and then returning the favor. Unlike rounds in beer-drinking circles, a couple of drams are enough to seal a friendship or to change the world. Your piece may be taken, but there's always time for another move… Tomorrow you'll feel dead beat? So what!

The stopper

Good whiskeys have a cork stopper, blends that are drunk more quickly have a screw cap. The cork makes a soft pop on opening and squeaks as it is replaced, the screw cap makes a metallic rasping sound – a subtle distinction.

Pouring pleasure

iskᵉy is **served** in small measures — a dram is poured in just one or two "glugs". It is a sound of **promise**, music to the ears of whiskᵉy drinkers and their guests. Full bottles glug all the re fervently, while old-fashioned, bulbous bottles make an altogether longer and louder noise n modern slimline ones. Consequently bottlers are increasingly returning to the old shapes. e luxurious, **sensual** sound of whiskᵉy being poured sets it apart from other spirits.

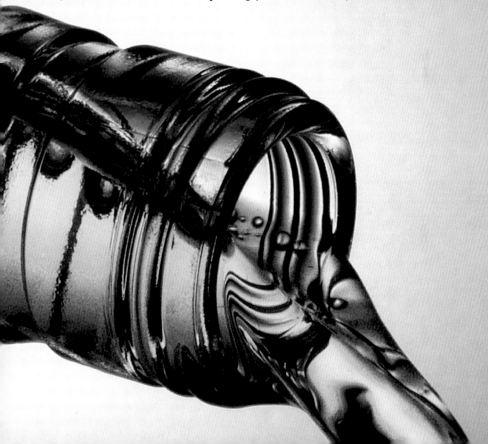

This way...

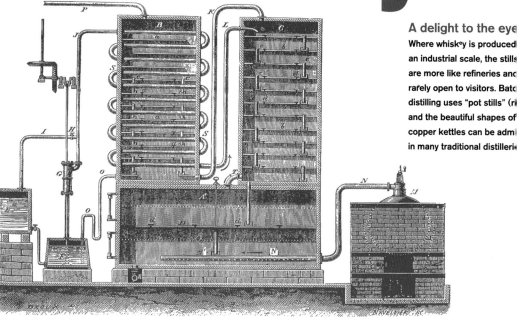

Since 1830 most whisk^ey^s have been distilled by means of a continuous, refinery-style proce
using a patent still, known as a **Coffey still**, after its inventor, or a **column still**, due to its sha
Perforated plates in the columns function as mini stills: hot steam from below meets the "distill
beer" that is being pumped in, and distils it. This technique made the mass production of **gr
whisk^ey^** possible, and opened the way for the creation of top-grade blends — combining gr
whisk^ey^ with higher-quality single malts from pot stills.

...or that

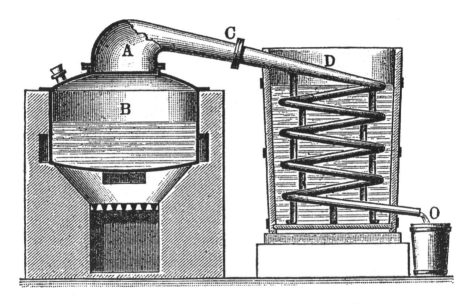

...e best whisk^ey in the world (a tiny proportion of the overall production) comes from such **pot ...ls**, traditional Irish or Scottish distilling apparatus with a copper pot for boiling and distilling. ...e flat, bulbous or pear shape of the still is different in every distillery and this, together with ...size, plays a crucial role in the character of the distillate which vaporizes in the coils of the **...ndensing worm**. For greater purity, the liquid is distilled subsequently in two pot stills; in ...and there are always three stills to guarantee that special **"triple-distilled"** quality.

DISTILLATIO.

In igne ſuccus omnium, arte, corporum   Vigens fit vnda,

Whisk^ey is nothing other than
aqua vitae

The early history of whisk^ey production is one of trial and error. While the Arabs had already mastered the technique of **distilling** low-proof alcohol in around 600 AD, the fact that distillates could be used to create an entirely new substance was still considered by outsiders as magic. As in illicit stills today, **inadequacies** in the alchemists' laboratory conditions resulted not in pure ethyl alcohols but in a rather nauseous **"medicine"**. This was the potent "water of life", in Latin "aqua vitae" and in Gaelic "uisge beatha" — or whisk^ey!

An open book
The ancient Arabs brought distillation to Europe — and used it to make a potent medicine.

potiſsima .

15

bootlegger
Also booter or bootie, an illicit distiller or seller of whiskey (1920s, USA)

kitchen
Illegal, usually domestic, distillery, also "alki cooker"

moonshine
Corn whiskey from an unlicensed still (1880s, USA)

mountain dew
Whiskey distilled illegally in the mountains, later a quirky brand from legal distilleries

rotgut
Poor-quality, cheap, originally illegal whiskey, also "panther piss"

potheen, poitín
Irish term for homemade whiskey distilled from any basic raw ingredients, especially potatoes, still practiced in remote areas

speakeasy
Originally a bar serving alcohol illegally, also "moonshinery" or "speaketeria", a more upmarket is a "class speak"

drinkable
Originally a bar serving alcohol illegally, also "moonshinery" or "speaketeria"

Big screen bootleggers' boun
During Prohibition a homespun whiskey, like this one bottled illegally by Frank McHugh a James Cagney in the 1939 film, "The Roarir Twenties", was known as "bath-tub liquor".

16

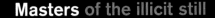
Moonshiners

The simple, though in most countries highly illegal, distilling process can be done at home and millions of people in the USA did it in response to the **National Prohibition Act** of 1920, using primitive distilling equipment in bathrooms, kitchens and garages. Smuggling flourished, as did the black market sale of alcohol and the running of illegal bars or **speakeasies** – all of which became a favorite topic in films. More Americans were drinking beer, whiskey and wine than ever before. Fashionable cocktails were disguised hard liquor and a last resort was to obtain a doctor's prescription. People took alcohol to parties in hoses around their waists, tucked into their garters, in hipflasks, or false books. Californian winegrowers, their livelihoods under threat, sold non-alcoholic musts and separate yeast so people could add sugar and ferment the wine illegally at home.

17

A stillman's job

A fine sense of judgement is an essential attribute for the stillman, who must observe the distillate from outside and take measurements as it passes through the "spirit safe" to decide when to draw off the **middle cut**, also known as the "heart of the run."

N°4 LOW

Distillers need no more than 4
ngredients

...ley

...ionally, barley is
...nated, dried and
...mashed. However,
...nciple any other
...of cereal can be
...to produce whisk...y.

Peat

The mash is imbued with
a hint of peat from the
water or, commonly for
Scottish malt whiskies,
lingers as an aroma in
the germinated barley that
is dried over a peat fire.

...er

...recise effect of
...ater still requires
...arch. It certainly
...nces the character
...e mash and also
...that of the diluted
..."strength" distillate.

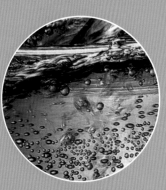

Yeast

Each distillery cultivates
its own yeasts to ferment
the sugars from the
starch in the barley
mash into a foaming
brew that is initially no
stronger than beer.

3 Once the still is producing nothing more than weak **"tails"** or **"feints"**, they are returned to the still and a new distilling process begins.

1 The first part of the run, the **"foreshot"** or **"head"** from the latest distillation, is too high in alcohol, oily and impure (due to all sorts of unwanted substances). The foreshot is therefore measured very precisely in the **spirit safe** by the **stillman** and sent back for re-distillation.

2 The middle part of the latest distillation is **the heart of the run.** This pure **middle cut** is directed by the stillman into the **spirit receiver tank** for as long as the measurements or the distillery's standards allow; depending on the distillery, this may be as low as 18% or perhaps as high as 60%.

3 After the usable middle cut from the freshly distilled **"baby whiskey"** come the **tails,** which have a lower alcohol content, smell quite different and contain large amounts of fusel oil, or the weaker **feints.** When this stage is reached the tails and feints, like the foreshot, are sent back for re-distillation by the stillman.

1 The process operates in a **cycle** and the unused parts of the second, and in Ireland the third, distillation are mixed into each new batch and re-distilled.

No2 WASH STILL
CONTENTS
15,920 LITRES

Just a few crucial minutes matter in the
Decision process

The final stage

In every distillery the internal pipes end up in a vat labeled like this one. Customs and Excise monitor strictly what arrives here as freshly distilled whiskey and is then sent from the full vat into the individual casks. Officially no samples may be taken, although the air is heavily permeated…

.to the vat!

This is where the freshly distilled **baby whisk**e**y** ends up. It is pumped from huge collecting vats into individual casks and, in the New World, may even be diluted at this stage. The casks then remain in the **warehouse** for a legally-defined minimum period and often much longer, although a young whisk e y with a high alcohol content tastes as powerfully aromatic as a smooth old grappa.

flavors from old barrels

e
e Scottish malts were
red in white wine barrels,
ture now appreciated by
connoisseurs and even
idered collectible.

gnac
rend for finishing, that
condary maturing in a
ent used cask, has seen
er cognac casks come
used for whiskey.

n
key has even been
red in rum barrels,
ver, this rather unusual
iment produced a
key that was greenish
or.

ble Wood
e whiskey is only fully
ed with the addition
ernal aromas, the
ing process deliberately
kes this by refilling the
into a second cask.

Oak has been used for many purposes, including centuries-old buildings, ships and furniture. But as cask wood it has such unique physical and chemical properties that it is not only wines that are drawn from the **"barrique",** the world's whiskeys rely on it too. **Oak wood** is quite breathable and is full of tannins, lipids and other aromatic substances that **interact** with any alcohol contained in the barrel. To facilitate this process of interaction, the insides of new and used barrels are **toasted** or, more intensively, **charred.** Connoisseurs claim that 60% to 70% of the character of a single malt comes from the oak wood. If barrels have previously contained other spirits, this prompts an **aromatic exchange** with the legacy of flavors in the cask's wooden sides. Using a second barrel is known as finishing and is indicated on the label with the words "double wood".

Sherry
Used sherry casks are the traditional but now expensive method used for maturing the first fill of whiskey and may be used for one or two refills.

Port
The more experimental distilleries favor port barrels as the best second-hand barrels, which produce a flavor known as "port-pipe".

Bourbon
Used bourbon barrels made from low-tannin American oak with a distinctive vanilla aroma are used in 90% of Scotch warehouses.

Madeira
Since finishing became fashionable, small, precious quantities of whiskey with a hint of sweetness have appeared on the market, matured in old Madeira casks.

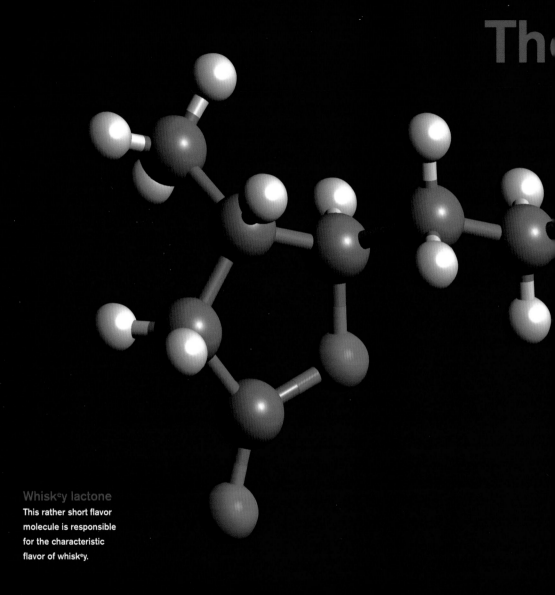

Whisk^ey lactone

This rather short flavor
molecule is responsible
for the characteristic
flavor of whisk^ey.

whisk^ey molecule

Enjoy your whisk^ey, shut your eyes and repeat the new mantra: "C nine, H sixteen, O two" — this is the chemical formula for **whisk^ey lactones.** Based on its structure, the typical whisk^ey flavor imparted by oak wood is also a "3-methyl-4-octanolide" or "5-butyl-4-methyl-dihydro-2(3H)-furanone". Break the ice at parties by telling people that the whisk^ey molecule is also known as "4-hydroxy-3-methyloctanoic acid gamma-lactone"! You could add that its molecular weight is 156.23. Lactones are internal esters of hydroxy acids and are so highly aromatic that their potency is only rivaled by musk. Of course, now the whisk^ey lactone molecule has been identified it has been isolated and **synthesized** — and vintners have already used these secret flavorings to create new "super wines" with the most amazing barrique flavor. However, they were caught because lactone can be detected. Let's hope the whisk^ey industry can resist the temptation.

Whisk^ey under the microscope

First it was a bit of fun, then it became an obsession at the microscopy laboratory at Florida State University: crystallizing pure whisk^ey and other drinks. The hardest layers of ice crystal glistened in the polarized light and as they began to melt, the crystals dissolved in brilliant rainbows of color. Research is in progress as to whether this can be used for identifying the various brands. In the mean time, the results illustrate the visual beauty of flavor.

Scotch

Scotch on the rocks

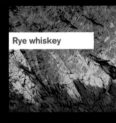
Rye whiskey

Jack Daniel's

Crown Royal

2%

of whisky evaporates from a wooden cask, no more is allowed by the British taxman to vanish in the warehouse as the "angels' share".

5%

is the amount of malt whisky in most of the cheapest supermarket whiskeys, the rest is more or less flavorless grain whiskey.

5,5%

of whiskey evaporates from a barrel of (pre-diluted) bourbon every year, after 6 years a third has gone (known as the "angels' third").

40%

abv (UK 70° proof, US 80° proof) has been the EU standard for all whiskeys since 1998, clearly these are diluted.

50%

expensive malt whisky at least is contained in good and luxury blends, in times of surplus production it may be considerably more.

51%

corn grain is the proportion required by law for the mash for American bourbon (it may often be 70%–90%).

57%

abv was equivalent to 100° proof in the UK until 1980 and is still equal to 114° proof in the USA.

68,5%

abv (US 137° proof) is the legal minimum for freshly distilled whiskey when it is poured into casks.

80%

of a blended whiskey in the USA can be neutral alcohol, which can make it cheaper but also more likely to cause a hangover.

100%

certainty about the age of a whiskey is only possible by analyzing acids that only form during maturing, indicated by receptor molecules.

BRUICHLADDICH

2001

196

ISLAY SINGLE MALT

Place of pilgrimage
Bruichladdich, on Islay, is Scotland's westernmost distillery and supplies traditional, non-peaty Scotch whisky chiefly to the mainland for use in the very best blends.

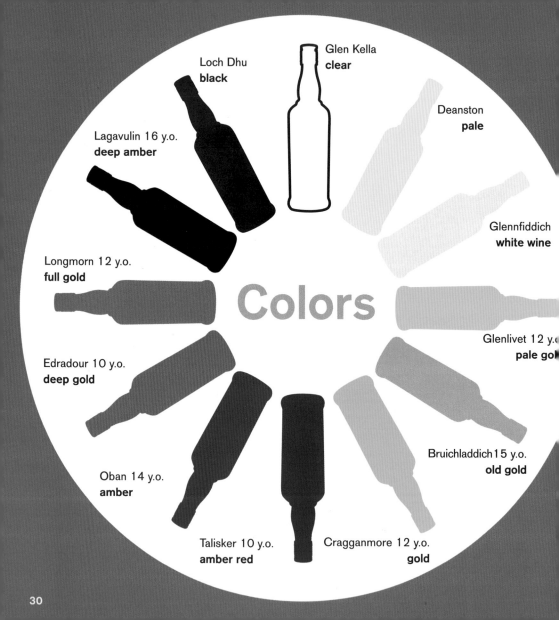

Loch Dhu
black

Glen Kella
clear

Deanston
pale

Lagavulin 16 y.o.
deep amber

Glennfiddich
white wine

Longmorn 12 y.o.
full gold

Colors

Glenlivet 12 y.o.
pale gold

Edradour 10 y.o.
deep gold

Bruichladdich 15 y.o.
old gold

Oban 14 y.o.
amber

Talisker 10 y.o.
amber red

Cragganmore 12 y.o.
gold

it is matured in the barrel, the clear, transpa- t young whisk^ey becomes darker in color r by year. The light-absorbing and simul- eously flavor-enhancing molecules are wn into the distillate from the sides of the ‹ **wood barrel**. Both distilleries and blend rketers place great value on the color con- tinuity of their malts, which has come to be expected by consumers. Most, although not all, adjust their whisk^eys with very small amounts of flavorless **caramel** to achieve the traditional or preferred tone. Some color the whisk^ey to create a dark, aged effect but this must then be indicated on the label.

ng for amber gold

whisk^ey color palette ranges from colorless (Glen Kella, re- lled after maturation) to black (Loch Dhu, due to cask charring caramelization). It is said that the darker the whisk^ey, the older herefore more valuable and expensive it is, but this is only a of thumb. The majority of colorful whisk^eys has seen additional mel to ensure the preferred shade is consistently maintained.

Nosing & Tasting

The language of the whisk^ey connoisseur is as flowery as that of the wine buff. After initially looking at the contents of the glass, both rely chiefly on their sensitive noses and spend a long time sniffing and deliberating over the aromas to identify a particular warehouse offering.

...ly gas chromatographs are more sensi...e than the **human** **...se** at distinguishing ...omas, but they can ...ly express their re...ts in bar graphs or ...zagging line graphs.

...master blenders ...d connoisseurs pre... to nose the alcoholic ...isk^ey bouquet as it ...es from a bulbous, ...ering glass, such as a sherry copita. Experts rub a few drops between the palms of their hands and sniff the warm flow of intensely aromatic molecules from their cupped hands. Next their **language skills** come into play to find a fitting decription for what their noses have experienced. Free rein is given to the imagination.

An individual's mood and prior knowledge may help (or hinder). First the **intensity** is analyzed (from slight to intense), followed by the character (from full to rich and even tremendous) and finally the overall impression — from dry or fruity to green, from medicinal to nutty or peaty, or even from sherry to sweet or vanilla. Then come additional impressions, such as whether the sample smells alcoholic or of banana, or floral with a heather note, or of honey. Sometimes the whisk^ey will **offend a sensitive nose,** if it has a mashy character or is overripe or has become woody through overmaturation.

1,500 years

The alcoholic panacea of the early monks became known as whisk°y and Irish and Scott experience eventually benefited the whole world through exports and shared distilling techniqu

500–600 AD missionaries from the Mediterranean bring the secret of distilling to Ireland **in 1276** Sir Robert Savage of Bushmills fortifies his troops before battle "with a mighty draught of uisce beathe" **in 1494** the Scottish Exchequer Rolls record "eight bolls of malt to Friar John Cor wherewith to make aqua vitae" **in 1608** Bushmills on Ireland's North Antrim coast is granted a license to distil whiskey by the River Bush and so the oldest distillery in the world is founded **in 1777** John Ritchie in Bradstown, Kentucky, or **in 1789** Baptist preacher Elijah Craig in Scott County, Kentucky, are said to have distilled the first bourbon in the USA **in 1791** a spirit tax is introduced in the USA and **in 1794** this gives rise to the bloodless "Whiskey Rebellion" in Pennsylvania and from then on leads to illicit distilling **1796** sees the death of Robert Burns, Scotland's national poet (born 1759), who wrote many

an apotheosis on whisky **in 1799** beer brewer Jo Molson distils the first Canadian whisky in Montr **in the 1820s** Alfred Eaton is thought to initi the "Lincoln County Process" for Tennessee wh key, filtering it through maple charcoal **in 18** distiller Robert Stein of Kilbagie near Edinburgh patents a continuous steam distilling process **in 1828** John Haig produces the first Scottish grain whisky in Cameronbridge, Fife, to make the malts go further **in 1830** Irishman Aeneas Coffey makes significant improvements to the continuous distilling method with his "patent" "Coffey still" and mass production of grain whisky a base whisky begins **in 1835** Scottish chem Dr James Crow reputedly uses the sour m method for the first time for his Old Crow bour **in 1853** Usher's OVG (Old Vatted Glenlivet), ma by Andrew Usher of Edinburgh, is the first comm cial whisky blend **in 1865** the grape phylloxe begin to destroy French vines **in the 1880s** cog

f whiskey

duction goes into decline and Scotch becomes gentleman's drink of choice **in 1866** the USA oduces a federal tax on whiskey, Jack Daniel's :omes the first registered distillery **in the 1880s** nitect Charles Chree Doig erects the first pagoda roof at the Dailuaine Distillery, later with his sons he constructs many more of these Scottish landmarks **in 1909** a British Royal Commission decides that "Scotch whisky" must be distilled and matured in Scotland and that grain spirit y also be called whisky **in 1915** the British nature Spirits (Restriction) Act stipulates a minim of two years' cask maturation **in 1916** the imum period for cask aging is set at three years **1920** the Eighteenth Amendment introduces l prohibition in the USA, leading (theoretically) 4 dry years; smuggling, illicit stills and mafia-run jal bars flourish **in 1923** Shinjiro Torii estables Kotobukiya (later Suntory) and **in 1929** the Japanese whisky, Shirofuda, goes on the market **in 1934** chemist and distiller Masataka Taketsuru sets up Nikka in Yoichi on Hokkaido's Shakotan peninsula to distil Japanese whisky **1933** sees the end of Prohibition in most parts of the USA **in 1939** Britain's war chest is swelled by an increase in the whisky tax **in 1948** the tax is ¾ of the cost of a bottle of blended whisky **in 1964** US Congress defines bourbon as: 51% corn, cask-aged for at least two years **in 1966** the Irish Distillers Company unites almost all of Ireland's whiskey producers (owned by Pernod Ricard since 1987), even taking over Bushmills **in 1970**, only Cooley remains independent **in 1973** Suntory builds the largest malt distillery in the world in Japan **in 1993** a Macallan whisky, distilled in 1926 and only bottled in 1986, fetches £15,000 at Christie's **in 1998** the EU stipulates that whisky must be a minimum of 40% abv **in 1999** Scotland alone exports 950 million bottles of Scotch whisky, thus 30 bottles per second are dispatched across a gratefully appreciative world…

The old
Irish

A fine prospect.
Monks who knew the alchemical secret of distilling
the "water of life" landed somewhere along Ireland's
900 miles of coastline – that's how the Emerald Isle
became whisky's native land.

Respect has been due to the Irish since the early Middle Ages as **Europe's first** whiskey distillers. However, they provoked the ire of the temperance movement in their own land, the envy of the nearby Scots and the export skullduggery of their opponents in London. By scorning blends and remaining fiercely loyal to their **"pure pot still"** and by losing a huge market during Prohibition in the US, Irish whiskey fell into a spiraling decline. Even Bushmills, the most traditional distillery, only survived through the **merger** with Irish Distillers. Yet the triple-distilled Irish nectar is still legendary.

Triple-distilled Irish blends:

Bushmills ("1608" 12-year-old, Black Bush up to 18 years old, also White Bush), Dun
Premium, Hewitts Whiskey, Inishowen (Cooley Distillery, a peaty rarity), Jameson (since 1
"1780", Crested Ten 8 to 15-year-old, Gold and limited edition "pure pot still" 15-year-old,
12-year-old Distillery Reserve), Kilbeggan (Locke Distillery, est. 1757, relaunched in 19
Locke's, Midleton Very Rare (limited edition), Millars Special Reserve, Mulligan, Murp
Premium, Old Comber (limited edition, Comber Distillery, closed 1953), Old Dublin, Pa
(since 1779), Power's (since 1791), Redbreast (also 12-year-old), Snug, Tesco Sp
Reserve, Tullamore Dew (since 1829, 3 to 6 and 12-year-old)

Triple-distilled Irish pure pot stills, or single malts:

Bushmills (since 1608, Original Bushmills 10-year-old, relaunched 1985, also 16-year
21-year-old Madeira Finish, 17-year-old Millennium Single Barrel, 12 to 14-year-old Ma
Distillers Reserve, also Black Bush and Triple Wood), Connemara (Cooley Distillery, relaunc
1996, 8-year-old, peaty, 40% abv, or "cask strength" 60.2% abv), Erin Go Bragh (i.e. Ire
forever, 6-year-old, remaining stock from the now closed Old Midleton Distillery), Locke's (s
1757, Cooley Distillery, 8-year-old, also available as special edition and in a ceramic cro
Tyrconnell (Cooley Distillery, since 1762, relaunched 1993, single malt and limited edition)
Irish single grain whiskey: Greenore (Cooley, 8-year-old)

Whiskeys spelt ey

Irish poitín

Illicitly distilled whiskey or "poitín" (English poteen) has been illegal for centuries, as for a long time was the sale of freshly distilled, immature distillates. However, this did not stop the Irish, either at home or in the New World, from setting up improvised pot stills in the remotest places and playing wild games of cat and mouse with the police. After all, a triple-distilled "baby whiskey" tastes wonderful, as full of character as grappa. Since 1997 the sale of this immature spirit has been legal, provided it is not described as "whiskey". Bunratty Potcheen – Irish New Make Spirit is the name of one 40% abv spirit that comes close to the old ideal. The English have also started distilling in the spirit of the Irish. Their Canterbury Knockeen – Irish Poteen is triple-distilled and is 45% abv. Indeed, the Gold Extra Strength (only for the duty free market) is a legendary 90% abv – almost equivalent to "straw rum"...

Moonshiners

The illicit distilling of poitín in primitive outdoor stills has a long tradition in Irish history. The Irish have a great love for the raw spirit and their bribing and tricking of the police has become the stuff of legends.

39

The epitome of whisky
Scotch

No other people are as strongly identified with their national drink as the Scots – and vice versa. They are proud of the ancient **document** proving that whisky was distilled by a monk in Fife as long ago as 1494. Many of today's 100 or so distilleries already existed as illicit stills in the same location centuries ago because of excellent water quality and nearby peat bogs. It was only with diminishing English repression and the lowering of the very high taxes that professional distilleries and a real **whisky industry** were established. From 1865 the grape phylloxera (vine pest) in France and resulting collapse in cognac production encouraged world-wide consumption of Scotch whisky. The new continuous distillation process meant milder blends could be made from the all too raw malts. For a long

time these malts, which differ consider from one distillery to the next and from Highlands to the Islands, were only use flavor the blends, which consisted ma of grain whisky. However, blend's **triumphal march** fered setbacks due to w wars, Prohibition in the U and a dangerous cycle of bo and periods of surplus pro tion that still persist today. Scottish news frequently cludes items about the closure or mothba of distilleries, as well as mergers and takeo by multinational companies. But none of has done any harm to Scotch, its origin maturation restricted to Caledonian soil. M taining **tradition** is still important, experim tation is limited and Scotch labels rer unmistakable.

...ttish...

...competition between
...land and Ireland for
...est "uisge beatha"
...s still ongoing. But
...he Scots who
...ously preserve the
...e of non-compro-
...g whisky and malt
...ty, as unmistakable
...ull of character as
...Highland cow.

Dalwhinnie

Scotland's highest distillery has nestled here in the furze-covered Highlands, 1,073 feet above sea-level, since 1897. Dalwhinnie means "meeting place" and once attracted cattle drovers and whisky smugglers. The distillery is famed for its very mild malts.

Single malt distilleries in the Highlands: Aberfeldy (1896), Arran (Isle of Arran, 1994), Ball (1790), Ben Nevis (1825), Blair Athol (1798), Clynelish, in Brora (1819), Dalmore (183 Dalwhinnie (1898), Deanston (1966), Drumguish (1990), Edradour (1825), Glen Dev (1962), Glen Elgin (1900), Glen Garioch (1798), Glen Moray (1897), Glen Ord (18 Glen Spey (1884), Glencadam (1825), Glengoyne (1833), Glenmorangie (1843), Glentu (1775), Highland Park (Orkney Islands, 1798), Inchmurrin (1966), Oban (1794), Fettercairn (1824), Pulteney (1826), Royal Brackla (1812), Royal Lochnagar (1845), Sc (Orkney Islands, 1885), Springbank (Campbeltown, 1828), Talisker (Isle of Skye, 183 Teaninich (1817), Tobermory (1795), and Tomatin (1897)

Single Malt Distilleries in Speyside/Highlands: Aberlour (1826), Ardmore (1898), Aultm (1895), Balmenach (1824–1993), Balvenie (1892), Benriach (1898), Benrinnes (183 Benromach (1898), Caperdonich (1897), Cardhu (1824), Craigellachie (1891), Cragg more (1869), Dailuaine (1851), Dufftown (1896), Glen Grant (1840), Glenallachie (19 Glenburgie (1810), Glendronach (1826), Glendullan (1897), Glenfarclas (1836), Glenfid (1886), Glen Keith (1958), Glenlivet (1824), Glenlossie (1876), Glenrothes/Glen Ro (1878), Glentauchers (1897), Inchgower (1872), Kininvie (1990), Knockando (189 Knockdhu/An Cnoc (1893), Linkwood (1825), Longmorn (1894), Macallan (183 Mannochmore (1971), Miltonduff (1824), Mortlach (1824), Singleton (1974), Speyb (1897), Strathisla (1786), Tamdhu (1896), Tomintoul (1964), and Tormore (1959)

Single Malt
SCOTCH WHISKY

Single malt distilleries on Islay and Jura:
Ardbeg (1798), Bowmore (1779), Bruichladdich (1881), Bunnahabhain (1883), Caol Ila (1846), Isle of Jura (Isle of Jura, 1810), Lagavulin(1816), and Laphroaig (1815)

Single malt distilleries in the Lowlands:
Auchentoshan (1800), Glenkinchie (1837) and Bladnoch (1817)

Silent stills — closed or pulled down but vintage bottlings still sought by connoisseurs and collectors who pay a lot of money for them:
Banff (1824–1983), Coleburn (1869–1985), Convalmore (1894–1985), Dallas Dhu (1898–1983), Glen Albyn (1846–1983), Glenesk (1897–1985), Glenflagler/Glen Flagler (1964–1985), Glenglassaugh (1875–1986), Glenugie (1875–1983), Glenury Royal (1825–1985), Imperial (1897–1998), Littlemill (1772–1994), Lochside (1957–1991), Pittyvaich (1974–1993), Port Ellen (1825–1983), Rosebank (1840–1993), Tamnavulin (1966–1995), and Tullibardine (1949–1995)

Unique character
The contents of each whisky barrel is unique and the flavor of the whisky is always slightly different, even in the next barrel in the warehouse, like here at Glenfarclas. Once the maturation peak is reached, the barrel is rolled off for single malt bottling, vatting or blending.

a brilliant
blend

Around 90 per cent of all Scotch whiskies are blends and are actually really a modern fashion. It was in the middle of the 19th century that **Andrew Usher** became the first person to **blend** widely differing and barely matured Scottish malt whiskies with the new, neutral tasting **grain whisky,** thereby creating the first milder brand whiskies. Wholesalers such as Walker, Dewar, Ballantine, and Chivas and distillery owners such as Haig backed this new trend and soon became wealthy **whisky barons** who established vast brand empires with their individual blend recipes. Master blenders guarantee continuity of flavor for decades, devising and creating the standard, premium and highly malty **deluxe blends** that are prized throughout the world.

John Walker

After blending teas and coffees in his grocer's shop (left), John Walker hit on the idea of doing the same thing with whisky. His son, Alexander, created the Johnnie Walker brand in memory of his father. Today experienced "noses" still create new blends from countless samples, as here with Cutty Sark (right).

Grant's Family Reserve (formerly Standfast, William Grant & Sons, also Ale Cask Sherry Cask Reserve), 100 Pipers (Chivas Brothers, since 1965), 500 Anniversary Bl (created by master blender Richard Paterson), Allt-A-Bhainne (Chivas Brothers, s 1975), Black Prince (also Select and Deluxe, 12, 17, 20 and 25-year-old), Black & W (since 1884), Black Bottle (with malts from the seven Islay distilleries, 10-year-old), Campbell, Cluny (since 1857, now only 12 or 17-year-old and Deluxe 21-year-o Compass Box (also Asyla, Eleuthera, Hedonism, 43% abv), Dunhill (since 1982, Gentleman's Speyside Blend, Old Master, Celebration Edition, in decanter, also Centenary Cask Edition), Glen Dowan (also 21 or 25-year-old), Glen Rosa, Haig & H Five Star, Hankey Bannister (also 12, 15 or 21-year-old), John Barr (since 1978, Special Reserve and Black), Langs (Supreme and Select), Loch Lomond (also Sir Blend!), Old Parr (popular in Japan, also Superior, Tribute, Elizabethan and Seasons, si the 1870s), Old Smuggler (since 1835), Queen Anne (Chivas, one of the oldest bran Queen Mary I (3, 5, 8 and 10-year-old), SS Pierce, Something Special (Chivas), Stewa Cream of the Barley, The Antiquary (named after a novel by Walter Scott, since 185 The Bailie Nicol Jarvie (named after a character in Walter Scott's "Rob Roy", since 18 The Claymore (since 1890), The Corriemhor, VAT 69 (since 1882, in Korea also Ex Whyte & Mackay (also High Strength and Tribute Decanter, 12, 15, 18, 21 and 30-year-old

Blends

The best known blends

Ballantine's (since 1827, also Royal Blue, Gold Seal, Founder's Reserve 1827, 12, 15, 17, 18, 19, 21 and 30-year-old, also Pure Malt), Bell's (8-year-old, also Extra Special, Decanter and Prince of Wales 50th), Chivas Regal (est. 1801, 12, 18 or 21-year-old, also Rare Old, Royal Salute, triple-blended, Revolve, Imperial Premium, and Century – a vatted malt made from 100 single malts), Cutty Sark (since 1923, also Emerald, Discovery, Golden Jubilee, 12, 18 and 50-year-old), Dewar's (since 1846, White Label No. 1 in the USA, also Ancestor Deluxe version), Dimple (12 or 15-year-old), Highland Queen (also Majesty, Grand Reserve, Supreme, and Queen of Scots, 12, 15 or 21-year-old), J & B (Rare, Reserve, Jet, and Ultima), Johnnie Walker (since 1908, Red Label – the number one Scotch world-wide – also Black, Gold, Green and Blue Label with up to 80% malt content), Teacher's Highland Cream (also Teacher's Royal Highland 12-year-old and Teacher's 50 with 50% malt), The Famous Grouse (also Gold Reserve 12-year-old), White Horse (named after the White Horse Inn in Edinburgh, since 1891)

Aiming high

The best bars pride themselves on offering 100 or more international whiskeys to suit the most varied tastes. The classic blends are stocked as a matter of course, but selected single malts are often also available.

49

Ancestral portraits

The Scottish Haigs have embodied the very model of a dis ling family since at least 1651. The su cess of their art wa considered a maste piece, as reflected early advertisemen

JOHN HAIG & CO. LTD
Messrs Haig & Haig Ltd
MARKINCH *Scotland*
GOLD LABEL
LIQUEUR SCOTCH WHISKY
DISTILLED AND BOTTLED IN SCOTLAND

A MASTERPIECE OF
THE DISTILLER'S ART

The Haig dynasty

re can be no two ways about it, the Haigs, came to England in 1033 with William the queror and soon made their way to Scot-l, are the oldest whisky distilling clan in the ld. Back in 1655 a Haig was called before church elders for operating his still on a **day.** When one John Haig married into illing circles in 1751, the family's career an in earnest. At the end of the 19th cen-, John Haig & Co, with their secret **blends,** e enjoying success with a range of Haig ds. The one which became the most known was their deluxe blend, "Dimple" "Pinch" in the USA). It is celebrated its "most famous bottle in the world", the three characteristic dimples, ated in around 1895 and long re Coca Cola.

Dimple
s celebrated blend in an ordinary bottle 1895, only then did ome famed for the les" or "pinches".

The man himself
Around 1900 the oldest whisky distillery in the world used a comic sketch of its patron in its adverts – the entire portrait is formed by the letters of Haig's name.

Corn

From corn to whiskey

The mash for US bourbon must contain at least 51% corn, which is what gives it its very different character and explains why it uses the distinctive spelling, "whiskey". The fact that bourbon is matured only in casks made from American oak gives bourbon its special flavor.

...ed whiskey

US whiskey owes its French name to **Bourbon County** in Kentucky, which was so christened in gratitude to France for its political support. Whiskey made from corn is thought to have been first distilled here in 1777, or 1789 at the latest. Even now barley is only added sparingly and in malted form to the "sour mash" for the beginning of the fermentation process. A **straight bourbon** must contain at least 51% corn and have a maximum alcohol content of 80% abv (160°). Sometimes rye is used instead of corn, in which case it is labeled "rye whiskey". This old production method almost died out, but the characteristic dry, bitter flavor has become fashionable again.

American whiskeys are not always barreled in pure form, but are often diluted immediately after distilling and before maturing. All bourbon is nevertheless then matured for a minimum of **two years** and always in fresh oak casks that impart the typical, sweet vanilla note. **Kentucky** is the distilling stronghold, while in **Tennessee** just two successful rival distilleries remain: Jack Daniel's and George A. Dickel. One of them produces "Tennessee Whiskey", while the other makes "Tennessee Whisky", without the "e", but they share one special feature – for at least a week, the freshly distilled whiskey is filtered through a layer of charcoal that absorbs foreign substances. This "charcoal mellowing" creates a cleaner, smoother flavor.

Ancient Age (also 90°, 100°, 107°, Ancient Ancient Age/Triple A or Ten Broom, 86° or 9
Barrel 107 (10-year-old, 107°), Basil Hayden's (8-year-old, 80°, recipe from 179
Blanton's (Single Barrel, Original, Silver Gold Edition, and Special Reserve, 80°, 93°, 9
or 103°), Booker's (Single Barrel, Special Barrel, 6 to 8-year-old, 121–127°), Bulleit (si
1830, also 90° and 101°), Evan Williams (in 1783 the first official distiller in Kentucky, a
Black Label, Green Label, Single Barrel, Single Barrel Vintage, also 4-year-old, 1783, Mas
Distiller's Select, 4 to 23-year-old with 86°–107°), Four Roses (Yellow, Black and Platin
Label and Single Barrel Reserve, also 86°), Jim Beam (Black, 7 or 8-year-old, also 86°, in
USA 90°, Gold Label 100° only for Australia, White 4 or 7-year-old, 80°), Kentucky (Gentlen
also 86°, 100° and Legend or Spirit – a Single Barrel version of Wild Turkey, 8-year-old, 10
Vintage 90°, Tavern also 100°), Knob Creek (Small Batch Bourbon by Jim Beam, 9-year-
100°), Maker's Mark Whisky (spelt without the "e", also Black Seal, Gold Seal Limited Editi
VIP Gold Top, Single Barrel Vintage, min. 6-year-old, 86°–101°), Old Charter (since 18
also Proprietor's Reserve, The Classic 90, Broom, 8, 10, 12, and 13-year-old, also 86°–10
Old Kentucky Rifle, Pappy Van Winkle's Family Reserve (20 or 23-year-old, 90.4°, 95.
Pennypacker, W. L. Weller (also Centennial, Special Reserve, Antique, Broom, Spring 19
7 to 19-year-old with 90°–107°), Wild Turkey (also Brown Label, Gold Label, Old No. 8 Bra
Rare Breed, Russell's Reserve, Kentucky Spirit, Broom, Barrel Proof, 6 to 12-year-old, also 86.
101°, 108.6°), Woodford Reserve (also Distiller's Select and distilled in "pot stills", 90°, 90.4

US Whiskey

Bourbon cousins

Old Rip Van Winkle (a "wheated bourbon", 10, 12 and 15-year-old, 90°, 90.4°, 107°), Old Williamsburg No. 20 (kosher whiskey, 3-year-old, 101°), RX Bourbon (by George A. Dickel, since 1983, bourbon filtered through charcoal with special caramel notes in the barrel, 6-year-old), Virginia Gentleman Small Batch Bourbon (by A. Smith Bowman, 80°, 90°)

Not bourbon

Early Times Old Style Kentucky Whisky (matured in used oak casks and so cannot be called "bourbon")

Straight ryes (with at least 51% rye and the traditional dry bitterness): Jim Beam Yellow Label, Old Overholt, Pikesville, Rittenhouse, Van Winkle, and Wild Turkey Rye

Single malts (very rare): McCarthy's Oregon Malt (Clear Creek Distillery, made using Scottish malt), Old Potrero (distilled using rye malt from San Francisco!, bottled at 13 months and 124°), Peregrine Rock (California Pure Malt Whisky made with peaty Highland barley, aged in bourbon casks)

Firing the filter charcoal

Only two Tennessee bourbons, Jack Daniel's and George A. Dickel, receive this special "purifying" treatment. For seven to ten days the whiskey is filtered through carefully charred maple charcoal. The result of this "charcoal mellowing" is a particularly clean-flavored and digestible whiskey

Same again, please!

"There is no such thing as a small whiskey!" Irish poet Oliver St. John Gogarty was speak
from the heart to all **men.** After all, first they distilled it, then smuggled it and once even stag
a rebellion in the USA on its behalf – for tax freedom and the right to distil it at home. Glass
glass they have learnt to endure their inferiority, with words of comfort from Compton Macken
"Love makes the world go round? Not at all. Whisky makes it go round twice as fast as love."

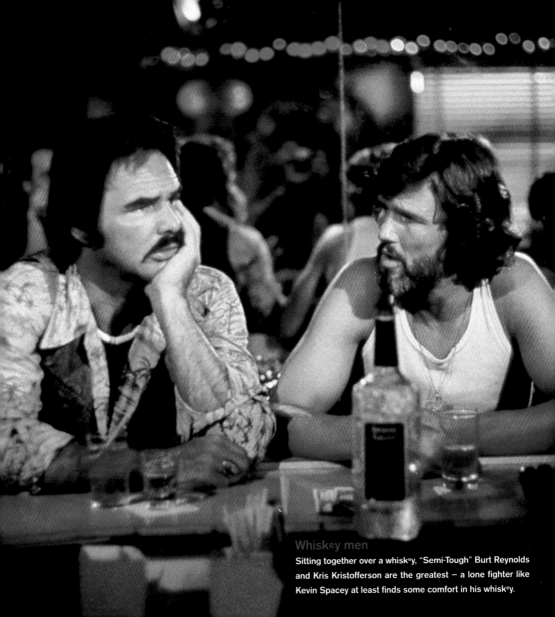

Whiskey men
Sitting together over a whiskᵉy, "Semi-Tough" Burt Reynolds
and Kris Kristofferson are the greatest – a lone fighter like
Kevin Spacey at least finds some comfort in his whiskᵉy.

S m a l

> **Peat:** the Scots claim that first-time drinkers receive the "kiss of life" fr[om] mighty Scotch whiskies like the Laphroaig or Lagavulin malts. "[You] either love it or you hate it." The phenolic, medicinal tone of pe[at] whisk^{e}ys is measured in ppm (parts per million). A 2003 Octom[ore] from Bruichladdich came up with 80.5 ppm (rather th[an] the usual 70 ppm), making it the peatiest single m[alt]. **Powder:** believe it or not there is such a thing [as] powdered whisk^{e}y, although the resulting clo[udy] liquid cannot be called "whisk^{e}y" because [the] carrier substance invented for powdering [by] German Professor Weidner remains in [the] drink. **Money:** old whisk^{e}y and spe[cial] bottlings are worth a flutter. In spr[ing] 2003 a 60-year-old Macallan was auc[tio]ned for £10,500, the previous year a 62-y[ear] old Dalmore fetched the record sum of £25,8[00]. **Misleading packaging,** since speculating has beco[me] such big business, amazing finds from long-gone[,] moth-balled distilleries, the so-called "silent stills", are forever popping [up]. Suspected forgeries of bottles from legendary distilleries, such as P[ort] Ellen, and bottlings from casks apparently "forgotten" by independ[ent]

Well, well, well…
Connoisseurs like to keep a firm grip on their glass and their specialist knowledge, which they are more than happy to share – the world of whisk^{e}y is full of fascinating facts.

t a l k

...ttlers appear out of the blue. The truth is in the drinking... **Long-lasting,**
...old whisk^{e}y can last for years in the dark after bottling – only
...it will damage it, which is why the more exclusive
...ttles come in boxes or metal cylinders. Sealed bottles
...m old shipwrecks have proved to contain surprisingly
...ll-preserved Scotch whisky even after 100 years or
...re. **Collecting,** probably the largest whisk^{e}y collection
...the world belongs to Giuseppe Begnoni of Bologna
...o has 15,000 brands and bottlings and between 40,000
...d 50,000 bottles, which he sometimes auctions over
...e internet. **Prohibition,** it still exists in some parts of the US.
...k Daniel's in Lynchburg cannot offer visitors anything
...onger than lemonade and any whiskey they buy may only
...sampled once they are over the county boundary.
...en the Scots had a dry spot: from 1922 to 1947 whisky
...ld not be sold in the fishing port of Wick, although
...ocal distillery (moth-balled 1930–1951) has distilled its
...cellent Old Pulteney whisky since 1826. **Good health,**
...C. Fields had the following medical advice: "Always carry a
...on of whisky in case of snakebite. And, furthermore, always
...ry a small snake. **„**

Whisk^ey &
cigars

Drink & smoke

Enjoying whisk^ey to the full means learning to take your time and the leisurely smoking of a cigar is an excellent accompaniment.

Part of the cultural history of Scotland's national drink is the triumphal march of the blends on London and from there across the British Empire. Whisky became the drink of choice in the **clubs** and what butlers served to **gentlemen** in private smoking rooms. Since then, male rituals, smalltalk and an expensive cigar have become an integral part of the whiskᵉy image. It has never been a drink for stress, but remains the **epitome of leisure** – lasting as long as a cigar…

The sweet, special
Canadian

distance from the "motherland" engen-
ed a healthy **disrespect** for Irish whiskey
Scotch in the Commonwealth country
Canada. Mill owners and beer brewers
n began to distil their own
sky. As long ago as 1799
first drops of liquid gold
ed from Canadian distil-
equipment. In the world's
rth most important whiskey nation,
labels and some bottle shapes
gest a louder and more colorful attitude.
ing Prohibition in the USA, Canadian
sky became legendary and even today
ericans still prefer it to their own bourbon.
ada's huge **exports** to the south for

US bottlers therefore also turn out rather
sweeter, suiting American tastes, and the
addition of up to 9.09% of fruit concentrates
and other **flavorings** is officially sanctioned.
This is why good bartenders all over the world
will ask **"Bourbon or Canadian?"** to
determine how sweet someone
likes their cocktails. The Canadian
whisky industry is now controlled
by a few large companies. They
sell whisky that has been matured
for at least three years either before or after
blending. However, the relatively new Glenora
distillery in Nova Scotia still resists the main-
stream and continues to distil malts like its
forebears in Europe.

mph!
g Prohibition in the USA, the Canadians made major inroads on
merican whiskey market. Back then Canadian whisky was used
secret cocktail ingredient and it is now bourbon's greatest rival.

The best-known Canadian whiskies:

Black Velvet (Barton Brands, at least 6 years old, top 20 brand world-wide), **Blackwc** (Shetland Isles), **Breton's Hand and Seal** (Glenora Distillery), **Bush Pilot's** (the only stra among the Canadians, also 13-year-old Private Reserve), **Canadian Club** (aged after blend since 1858, also Broom, Classic/Classic 12-year-old and Reserve, 6, 10 and 12-year-o **Canadian Company** (only in Canada and Taiwan, 4 and 10-year-old), **Canadian G** (3-year-old, exclusively exported to the UK), **Canadian Mist** (by Brown-Forman, successful in USA as 3-year-old, otherwise 4-year-old, also Broom and Special Reserve) **Canadian O.** ("Original Fine Canadian", 6-year-old, 8-year-old for export), **Captain's Table, Crown Rc** (the "Canadian Macallan", created in 1939 on the occasion of a visit by the British Royals, a Broom and 12-year-old Special Reserve), **Forty Creek Barrel Select, G. P. Miller, Gibso** (Finest 12-year-old and Sterling Version), **Gooderham and Worts** (since 1837), **Lot No.** (Canadian pot still, a rare whisky made from a malted rye mash), **MacNaughton** (by Bar Brands), **Maple Drop, McGuinness Old Canada, Order of Merit, Pike Creek** (matured port barrels), **Royal Canadian, Seagram's "83"** (since 1883, probably the oldest Canad whisky blend), **Silk Tassel** (27% and 40% abv), **(Seagram's) V.O.** ("Very Own" since 19 also Broom, Gold and Light, 30% abv)

Canadian single malts:

Blackstone (malt whisky made from malted grains, 8-year-old), Glen Breton (malt whisky from the Glenora Distillery which opened in 1990, only 500 numbered bottles from a bottling on 31 October 2000), Glen Ogopolo (malt whisky, sold exclusively in Japan)

Canadian Whisky, exclusively for the US market

Canada House
Canadian Host
Canadian Hunter
Canadian LTD (Barton Brands)
Canadian Province
Canadian Springs
Canadian Supreme
Crown Royal Limited Edition
Five O´Clock
Jenkins
Lord Calvert (Jim Beam)
Windsor Supreme (Jim Beam)
Northern Light

Kicking up a stink about drink

During Prohibition, smuggling flourished along the border with the USA, but the FBI lost the battle. The penchant established for the milder "Canadian" later helped it achieve the dominance it still enjoys in the USA.

65

Respect

Japan is home to the largest malt dis-
lery in the world and the country's o
dozen or so distilleries respect and
celebrate the Scottish art of distillin
and blending. Among Japanese men
expensive whisky enjoys cult status
In fact, together with so-called "sec
class whisky", it makes up the majo
of spirits sales.

ce 1973 the "Japanese Highlands" have
en home to the world's largest distillery. It
ongs to Suntory and boasts 24 pot stills.
mpany founder Torii initiated Japanese
isky production in 1929 with Shirofuda.
day whisky has an exalted status in Japan
d is drunk with water as "mizuwari" to
company food. The Japanese are partic-
rly fond of a whisky at the end of the
rking day in special bars from their own
sonal bottles. The price is high and the
lity undisputed. Japanese whisky is
tured for three years, like its role model
otch, but its low-peat mildness is in per-
t harmony with the Japanese way of life.
ly alliances and shares in Scottish pro-
ction meant whisky giants Suntory (60%
rket share) and Nikka could guarantee
pplies for their 12%–15% Scotch whis-
blends. Even Japanese single malts are
coming increasingly popular.

Melodious sound

As the Japanese word for whisky contains more "ee" sounds than
"cheese", a cry of "uisuki" can often be heard as photographers
exhort their subjects to smile. Similarly pleasing to the ear is the word
"mizuwari", meaning "broken water," which is "uisuki" diluted with water.

heese = uisuki

When they fancy a tipple at the Cho Oyu base camp, these travelers can crack open a **local whisky.** Gone are the days when whisky was only distilled in a few, generally colder countries. Nowadays everywhere, from traditional wine-growing countries to tropical regions, they produce their own brands. Spain is establishing itself, New Zealand and Australia are experimenting, and Austria has its oat whisky. There are malts from Brittany, as well as Switzerland and Germany. Meanwhile, **India's** national whisky has become a mass-produced drink with a wide range, sometimes blended with imported Scotch and sweetish to taste. However, the EU considers Indian whiskies to be exotic distillates made from sugar-cane molasses and officially defines them as **rum.** The more "authentic" Nepalese whisky bears the name of the legendary peak.

A whisky o

Promising brand

Even in Katmandu, on the "roof of the world", whisky is distilled. "Mount Everest" is produced with Scottish assistance.

A sweeter way with Whiskey

Liqueur

In spite of their sweetness, whiskey liqueurs are also popular with men. Centuries ago the Scots used malt, honey and herbs to make whisky palatable. **"Drambuie"** is Gaelic for "the drink that satisfies" and the brand name of the oldest whisky liqueur – supposedly the personal liqueur of **Bonnie Prince Charlie,** last of the Stuart (Scottish) pretenders to the British throne. He is said to have given the recipe to the MacKinnons in 1746, in gratitude for their aid in his flight from Scotland. Many distilleries and brands, even Johnnie Walker, have produced a whisky liqueur. However, none have equaled the success of the Irish cream liqueur, **Bailey's,** which since 1974 has outstripped all its rivals, even the older established **Irish Mist.** Younger drinkers especially are unembarrassed about their passion for such sweet liqueurs as an **aperitif with ice** or sophisticated **digestif** with dessert. Cocktails with whisky liqueurs, such as "Rusty Nail", are also popular. The "Prince of Wales" whisky became a nostalgic drink from 1986, recreating the **herbal refinement** of an earlier age.

Southern Comfort

Southern Comfort, liqueur of the Southern states, became a cult drink, but only the "Reserve" contains bourbon. Peach and lemon flavorings and vanilla notes from cask maturing supplement the neutral alcohol.

No thanks...

Ice cold

Connoisseurs always drink good whiskeys without ice. Drunk on the rocks on a hot day or by the thirsty, it is pleasing to the eye and the clinking ice cubes promise cool refreshment. The further from Europe, the more ice in the tumbler, especially in the USA.

GLEN GRANT

Yes, please!

...sk strength whisk[e]y has such a high alcohol con-
...t that, although beguiling to the nose, it will numb
...e tastebuds too quickly. This is why connoisseurs
...**ute** it with a **dash of soda water,** unobtrusively
...owing the bar tender with one or more
...**gers** how much or how little pure water they
...nt in the glass. Gentlemen used to indicate
...s with one of the three edges of a match-
...x, which developed into a discreet ritual.
...cionados rarely ask for ice because
...e cold tends to **dull** the senses. Only
... long drinks in the summer are **ice**
...**bes** containing whisk[e]y sometimes
...e-frozen to avoid over-dilution.

...ystal clear

...noisseurs draw out the whisk[e]y flavors
...just a little water and by preference
...se Scottish spring water to guarantee
...   pleasure.

Scotch classics

Affinity, Scotch Manhattan
Scotch, white and red
vermouth + orange or
Angostura bitters
Sandy Collins
Scotch, lemon juice,
soda + sugar syrup
Scotch Fizz
Scotch, chilled champagne
+ strawberries
Whisky Soda, Floater
Scotch, soda

Canadian classics

Manhattan
Canadian, red vermouth +
Angostura bitters, cherry
Manhattan Dry
Canadian, dry vermouth +
Angostura bitters, olive
Manhattan Sweet
Canadian, red vermouth
+ white curaçao, orange
bitters

Oriental

This was created with old Glenfiddich and
is flavored with ginger and orange peel.

Whisky-Cocktails

cktails with Scotch: **Bobby Burns** (Scotch, red or dry white vermouth + Bénédictine), arly's Cocktail (Scotch, apricot brandy + lemon juice + orange bitters), **Churchill** (Scotch, vermouth + curaçao triple sec, lemon juice), **Derby Fizz** (Scotch, soda + curaçao, lemon, dered sugar, raw egg), **Green Mist** (Scotch, crème de menthe + lemon juice), **Highland** oler (Scotch, ginger ale + lemon juice, Angostura bitters), **Highland Fling** (Scotch, amaretto, ger ale), **Highland Special** (Scotch, French vermouth, orange juice + nutmeg), **Hot Scotch** ddy (Scotch, boiling water, lemon juice + Angostura bitters, honey, cloves), **Lord Byron** cotch, orange liqueur, red vermouth + Angostura bitters), **Mint Cooler** (Scotch, soda + white me de menthe), **Purple Heather** (Scotch + cassis), **Rob Roy** (Scotch, red vermouth + gostura bitters), **Rusty Nail** (Scotch, Drambuie), **Scottie** (Scotch, pineapple juice, passion t juice + peach liqueur, grenadine), **Sweet Lady** (Scotch, white crème de cacao, peach ndy), **Sweet Science** (Scotch, orange juice + Drambuie), **Whisky Fizz** (Scotch, lemon e, soda + sugar syrup), **Whisky Mac** (Scotch, ginger wine), **Winter Warmer** (Scotch, brown jar, cloves + stick of cinnamon, lemon and orange peel)

cktails with Canadian: **Boston Flip** (Canadian, port + sugar syrup, cream, egg yolk), oklyn (Canadian, dry white vermouth + maraschino), **Canadian Horse's Neck** (Canadian, ger ale + Angostura bitters), **Canadian Old Fashioned** (Canadian + Angostura bitters, jar), **Canadian Sour** (Canadian, soda + lemon juice, sugar syrup), **Canadian Summer** anadian, soda + white crème de cacao, green crème de menthe), **Canadian Whisky Flip** anadian, cream + sugar syrup, egg yolk), **Captain Collins** (Canadian, lemon juice, soda sugar syrup), **Mounty** (Canadian, pineapple juice, lemon juice + grenadine), **Toronto** (Cana- n, Fernet Branca + sugar syrup, Angostura bitters)

Whiskey cocktails

Cocktails with bourbon: **America** (bourbon, lime juice + grenadine, lime peel), **Bourb**
Dream (bourbon, apricot brandy, orange juice), **Colonel Collins** or **John Collins** (bourb
lemon juice, soda + sugar), **Continental Sour** (bourbon, grenadine, lemon juice + red wine,
white), **Cowboy Cocktail** (bourbon, cream), **Dixie Julep** (bourbon + powdered sugar), **4th**
July (bourbon, apricot brandy, lemon and orange juice), **Frisco Sour** (bourbon, Bénédict
lemon juice), **Godfather** (bourbon, amaretto), **Kentucky Bourbon** (bourbon, Bénédic
+ cocktail cherry), **Kentucky Cocktail** (bourbon + pineapple juice), **King's Cross** (bourb
red vermouth + Bénédictine), **Lafayette** (bourbon, dry vermouth, Dubonnet + Angostura bitte
Manhattan Perfect (bourbon, white and red vermouth), **Monte Carlo** (bourbon, Bénédic
+ Angostura bitters), **New Yorker** (bourbon, lemon juice + grenadine), **New York**
(bourbon, port, cream, sugar syrup + egg yolk), **Old Pale** (bourbon, Campari + lime juic
Tennessee (bourbon, maraschino liqueur, lemon juice), **Waldorf Astoria** (bourbon, port, su
syrup, milk, cream + egg yolk, nutmeg), **Yankee Dutch** (bourbon, brandy, curaçao tri
sec, vodka), **York** (bourbon, red vermouth + Angostura bitters)

Cocktails with Irish whiskey: **Brainstorming** (Irish + Bénédictine, dry vermouth), **Camero**
Kick (Irish, Scotch + almond syrup, lemon juice), **Cherry Blossom** (Irish, lemon juice, grenadi
soda + egg white), **Everybody's Irish** (Irish, crème de menthe + Chartreuse), **Gloom Li**
(Irish, lemon juice, sugar syrup + egg white), **Irish Blessing** (Irish, Irish Cream), **Irish Bloss**
(Irish, soda + lemon juice, grenadine, egg white), **Irish Orange** (Irish, lemon juice, lime ju
+ grenadine), **(Wild) Irish Rose** (Irish, lemon juice + grenadine), **One Ireland** (Irish + wh
crème de menthe, vanilla ice cream + milk), **Whiskey Twist** (Irish + lemon juice, cherry bran
raspberry syrup)

Bourbon classics

Bourbon Highball
Bourbon, ginger ale or cola
or soda
Golden Nail
Bourbon, Southern Comfort
Mint Julep
Bourbon, sugar syrup
+ soda, mint
Old fashioned
Bourbon, pure water
+ Angostura bitters, cube
sugar
Whiskey Sour
Bourbon, lemon juice, sugar
syrup + Angostura bitters

Irish classics

Irish Coffee
Irish, hot coffee + brown
sugar, lightly whipped
Mike Collins
Irish, soda,
lemon juice + sugar

Classic Mint Julep
Here mixed with Jack Daniel's, the mintiness
smoothly sweetened.

Whisky wisdom and whiskey wis

Age is the length of time a whisk^ey has matured in an oak cask, the minimum period for aging is two years (for bourbons) and three years (in Ireland, Scotland, Canada, and Japan).

Angels' share is the whisk^ey that evaporates in a year from a maturing cask, usually 2%. In the USA dilution after barreling and higher warehouse temperatures mean it may often be 5.5%, or 33% in 6 years, hence also "angels' third".

Barley is the most important ingredient used in whisk^ey distillation in Ireland, Scotland and Japan.

Blending is the art of combining different types of whisk^ey to create a brand, it is always the youngest whisk^ey in the blend that determines what year appears on the label.

Bourbon is the main US-American whiskey, made from a mash with at least 51% corn and always matured in new oak casks to give the woody vanilla notes. The USA also produces rye whiskey and Tennessee sour mash whiskey.

Canadian is light, sweetish, usually blended whisky, containing a maximum of 9.09% added flavorings; the use of different grains means the types vary considerably.

Cask strength indicates the high alcohol content of undiluted whisk^ey bottled straight from the barrel.

Coffey/patent/column/continuous still is the twin-columned "refinery" for continuous distilling in large quantities.

Copita is the bulbous, tapering sherry glass that is considered the best for nosing and tasting whisk^ey.

Corn Whisk^ey is a specialty of the Southern states, r... of no less than 80% corn grain (UK English "ma... In the UK, grain whiskies are made of a mixed r... of cereals such as barley (for malts), rye, oats, w... or maize.

Dram is the Scottish word for a tot of spirit, it is also a... of whisky, known elsewhere as a "goldie", a "nip" "slug". A "wee dram" is a tempting invitation.

Finishing is the secondary maturation used to roun... the flavor of the whisk^ey in another cask which previ... contained a different drink. This flavoring process... recently become popular, the label then bears the le... "double wood".

Grain whisk^ey is a neutral spirit distilled continuou... a patent still and made from various types of grain. It al... makes up the largest share of a blend, is only very e... sionally "aged" and sold as "single grain".

Indian whisky is distilled in vast quantities and is also blended with imported Scotch. However, save for a few exceptions, it is defined by the EU not as a whisk^ey but as a distillate of sugar-cane molasses.

Irish whiskey is now less often the product of a traditional pot still. It is usually a blend of triple-distilled malt and grain whiskeys.

Japanese whisky is a light whisky, distilled as malt and grain varieties following the Scottish model and also blended with imported Scottish whiskies.

whisky is traditionally distilled in pot stills from
inated, often peaty barley malt.

iage describes the harmonious blending of distillates
rge vat; the blend is then left to stand for a few weeks
e bottling.

is used for casks because it contains substances
as lactones) that, on contact with alcohol, prompt
chemical reactions and enhance flavors. However,
ss lactones and over-maturation can cause whiskeys
come "woody".

whisky is made in the Austrian Alps.

is contained in the water and in the smoke used to
e malt, thereby enhancing flavor and character, espe-
in Scottish whisky.

t still is the name of the traditional copper stills used
or batch distillation; the size and shape of the still and
the "lyne arm" (pipe leading to the condenser)
have an inexplicable but unique effect on the
character of the distillate.

Poteen (Irish "poitín") is illegally distilled Irish
whiskey, often with a very unusual flavor (all
sorts of ingredients are used), uncontrolled
alcohol content, no maturation but focus of
great ceremony. Nowadays it is even marketed
– as "new spirit".

Proof is now (since 1980) only used in the USA
to denote the strength of alcohol in degrees (°), as
a rule of thumb: proof divided by 2 = % abv, e.g.
80° = 40% abv.

Scotch whisky is a protected designation of origin for
Scottish whisky distilled in Scotland and matured there for
at least three years.

Single malt describes any whiskey with its own unique
character from a single distillery. Most are "vatted malts",
blended by distilleries from their own malts, but the best
ones are "single cask malts", bottled from just one cask.

Slainté! is the Gaelic word for "Cheers!" and means
"health" or "well-being". "Slainté mhath, slainté mhor" basic-
ally means "good health!"

Sour mash is the US-American technique of adding
some of the working-yeast from the previous batch to the
fermenting vessel to ensure the consistent character of the
resulting whiskey. It does not taste sour.

Tennessee Whiskey is made using the Lincoln County
Process, whereby the distillate is filtered for 7–10 days
through maple charcoal (charcoal mellowing).

Uisce beathe is Scottish Gaelic for aqua vitae (water of
life) and eventually became "whiskey".

Vatted malts are single malt whiskies created by combining and vatting several single malts of one distillery for a
fully rounded flavor.

Whiskey is the spelling used for Irish whiskeys and American bourbons and their blends.

Whisky is the international spelling for distillates made from
beer-like barley mashes – except in Ireland and the USA.

Whiskey-liqueurs are whiskeys that are sweetened with
sugar and flavored with herbs, lemon essences or just
cream and contain 17% to 40% abv.

So long...

Your love of whisk^ey must have begun long ago or have always been with you, otherwise you would not have got this far. And you can continue to develop this love through tasting and technical talk, either on visits to distilleries or in specialty shops. Whisk^ey can be explored "horizontally" (geographically, by region) or "vertically" (by year and bottling). However you approach your research, it is bound to be a pleasure. Cheers!

Web of knowledge

www.smws.com

www.whiskyweb.com

www.thewhiskysite.com

www.whisky.com

www.maltwhiskytrail.com

www.classicwhiskey.com

www.straightbourbon.com

www.canadiandistillers.com

www.thewhiskystore.de

www.whisky-world.com

Photo credits

The editor and publishers would like to thank the following for permission of reproduction and their friendly support:
c. = center, ri. = right, l. = left, t. = top, b. = bottom
AKG 39; Bruichladdich 28; Bushmills 18, 19 t.l., 19 b.ri., 21/22, 36; Cutty Sark 46/47; defd 8 t. (2), 8 c.l., 8 b. (2), 8/9, 16/17, 56, 57, 65; Diageo Germany 14/15, 22/23 (Ulrich Kerth), 30, 35 l., 40, 42/43; Dimple 50, 51 ri.; dpa c.ri.; Drambuie 4; Florida State University 27 ri., (5); Glenfarclas 34 l., 45, 80; Glenfiddich 74; Glen Grant 72; Lutz Hiller 6/7, 10 b., 10/11, 60/61, 70/71, 71 t., 73; Ireland Tourism Information 36/37; Jack Daniel's 55,77; Jim Beam 22 l.; Johnnie Walker 22 ri., 32, 33 l., 46 b.; Oscar's 49; Redaktionsbüro Pini 12, 13, 19 t.ri., 19 b. l., 34 ri., 41, 51 l., 58, 59, 63, 66, 78/79; Stockfood 52/53; Stone 68/69; The Image Bank 62; Volkmar Vill 26/27; Tom Wolf 15 b., 33 ri., 68

Special thanks for photos and many a good hint: Allied Domecq Deutschland, Allied Domecq Esp Bacardi, Borowski Communications, Horst Jürg and Elke Bewarder, BORCO brands import, Bu Marsteller, Connaisseur Kommunikationsberatur c.t.b., Dalmore Distillery, Destillerie Weidenauer, Diageo Deutschland, Eggers & Franke, Glasfirn Giessen, HWG Hanseatische Weinhangelsgesel Highland Water, Höppner Graphik Contor, Diete Kirsch, Horst Lüning, Maxxium Germany, Perno Ricard Germany, RASTAL, Schlumberger, Segn PR, semper idem ° Underberg, Signatory/Andre Symington, The Scotch Malt Whisky Society, pr Eckhard Weidner and his team

The editor and publishers have made every effort the production process to trace the owners of the to all other pictures. Individuals and organizations may not have been contacted and to whom the ri pictures used in this publication belong, are asked contact the publishers.